MAKING SCIENCE WORK

Electricity
and
Magnetism

TERRY JENNINGS

Illustrations by
Peter Smith and
Catherine Ward

RSVP

**RAINTREE
STECK-VAUGHN**
PUBLISHERS
The Steck-Vaughn Company

Austin, Texas

Published by Raintree Steck-Vaughn Publishers, an imprint of Steck-Vaughn Company

A Mirabel Book

Produced by Cynthia Parzych Publishing, Inc.
648 Broadway, New York, NY 10012

Designed by Arcadia Consultants

Printed and bound in Spain by International Graphic Service

1 2 3 4 5 6 7 8 9 0 pl 99 98 97 96 95

Library of Congress Cataloging-in-Publication Data
Jennings, Terry J.
    Electricity and magnetism / Terry Jennings: illustrations by Peter Smith and Catherine Ward.
        p.   cm. — (Making science work)
    Includes index.
    ISBN 0–8172–3957–X
    ISBN 0–8172–4250–3 (softcover)
        1. Electric apparatus and appliances—Juvenile literature.
    2. Electricity—Experiments—Juvenile literature.   3. Magnetism—Experiments—Juvenile literature.
[1. Electricity—Experiments.   2. Magnetism—Experiments.   3. Experiments.]   I. Smith, Peter, 1948- ill.
II. Ward, Catherine, ill.   III. Title.   IV. Series: Jennings, Terry J. Making science work.   95–6203
TK148.J52 1996   CIP
621.3—dc20   AC

Key to Symbols

 "See for Yourself" element

 Demonstrates the principles of the subject

 Warning! Adult help is required

 Activity for the child to try

PHOTO CREDITS
Art Director's Photo Library: 20
B & U International Picture Service: 8 bottom, 10 left
Birmingham International Airport PLC: 29
© Jonathon Eastland: 26 right
Jennings, Dr. Terry: 7 top and bottom, 8 top, 10 right, 26 left
© Superstock Inc.: 17
VME Construction Equipment GB Ltd, photo by Grahame Miller: 28

**Warning: It is safe to experiment with flashlight batteries.
Never play with other electricity sources. They could kill you.**

Contents

Electricity Everywhere

We use electricity every day. We use it to light our homes and schools. Many people use electricity for cooking and heating. Electricity keeps our food cool. Electricity powers our televisions, radios, and stereos. Electricity powers our computers. Electricity makes streetlights work. Even some trains are electric. How many electrical things have you used today?

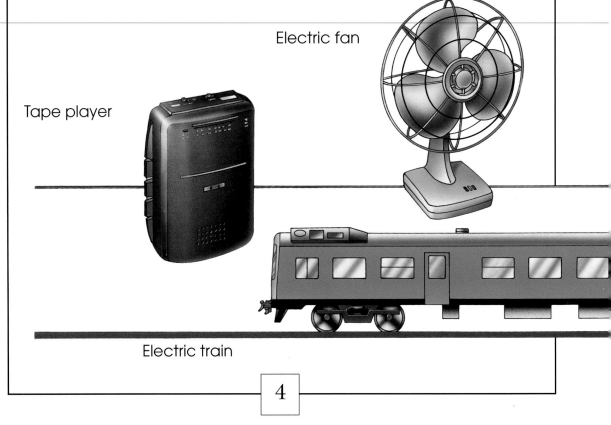

Electric fan

Tape player

Electric train

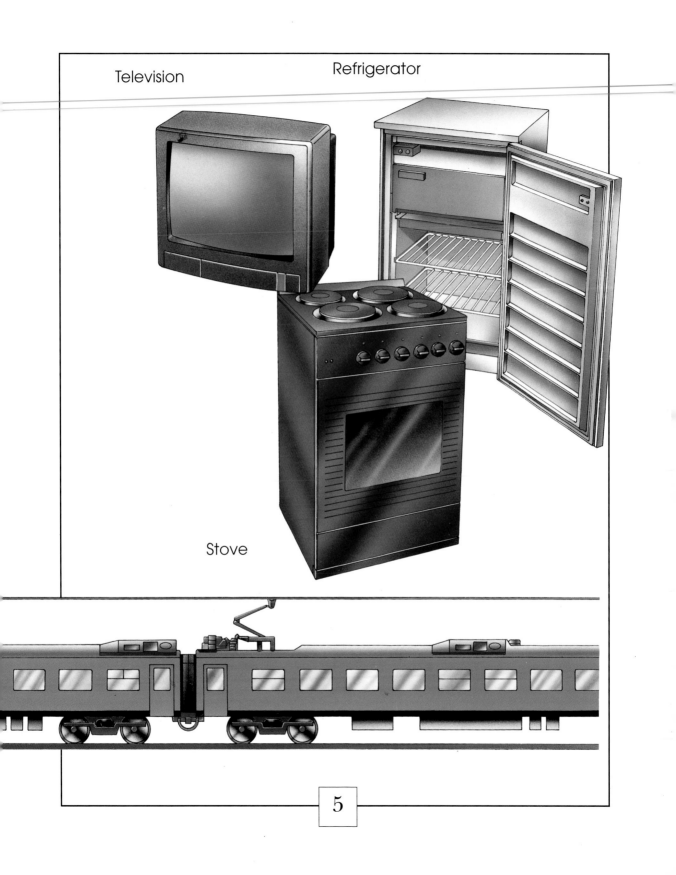

Television

Refrigerator

Stove

Power Plants

Most electricity is made in a power plant. Some power plants burn coal, oil, or gas. A few power plants use a fuel called uranium. All these fuels produce heat. The heat turns water into steam. The steam travels through pipes to a turbine. The turbine is like a big fan. The steam pushes the blades of the turbine. The steam makes the blades spin very fast. As the turbine spins, it turns a machine called a generator. This produces electricity.

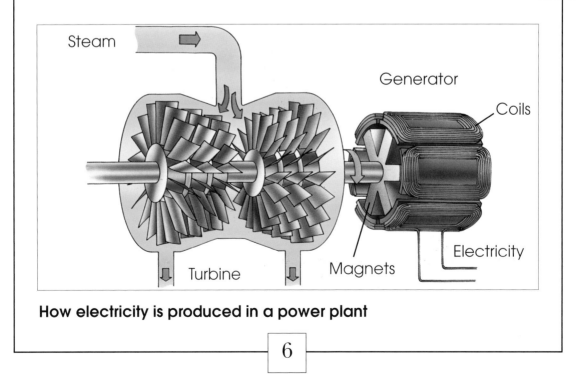

Steam

Generator

Coils

Electricity

Magnets

Turbine

How electricity is produced in a power plant

A coal-fired power plant

The electricity travels to factories, homes, and stores that use it. Electricity travels through thick, heavy wires. These are called cables. The cables are held high up on utility poles or pylons. Sometimes the cables are buried under the ground.

Electricity pylon

Electricity Without Fuels

There are other ways to produce electricity. Special windmills can produce electricity. The wind pushes against the blades of the windmill. It makes them turn. The moving blades turn the generator. This produces electricity.

A wind generator

Solar power plants change the heat or light from the sun into electricity. To do this they use mirrors or solar panels. Very small solar panels are used to power watches and calculators.

A solar power plant

A hydroelectric power plant uses falling water to produce electricity. The water comes from a huge lake called a reservoir. The water rushes down big pipes. At the bottom of each pipe is a turbine. The water spins the turbine. As the turbine spins, it turns the generator. This produces electricity.

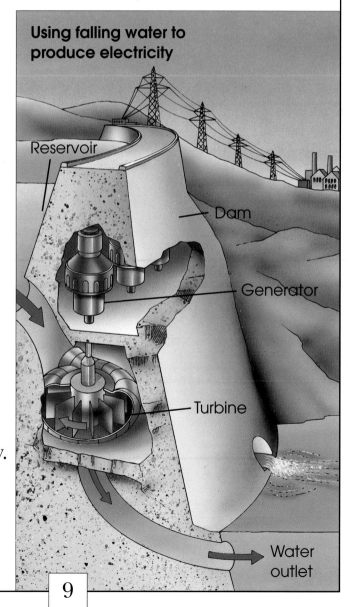

Using falling water to produce electricity

Reservoir

Dam

Generator

Turbine

Water outlet

Batteries

Not all our electricity comes from power plants. A flashlight uses batteries. A battery has chemicals in it. When a flashlight is switched on, the chemicals produce electricity. This lights the bulb. When the chemicals are used up, a battery cannot produce any more electricity. The battery is then thrown away. Some batteries can be recharged with electricity. Then they can be used again. A car battery can be recharged with electricity.

A car battery

A flashlight with its batteries

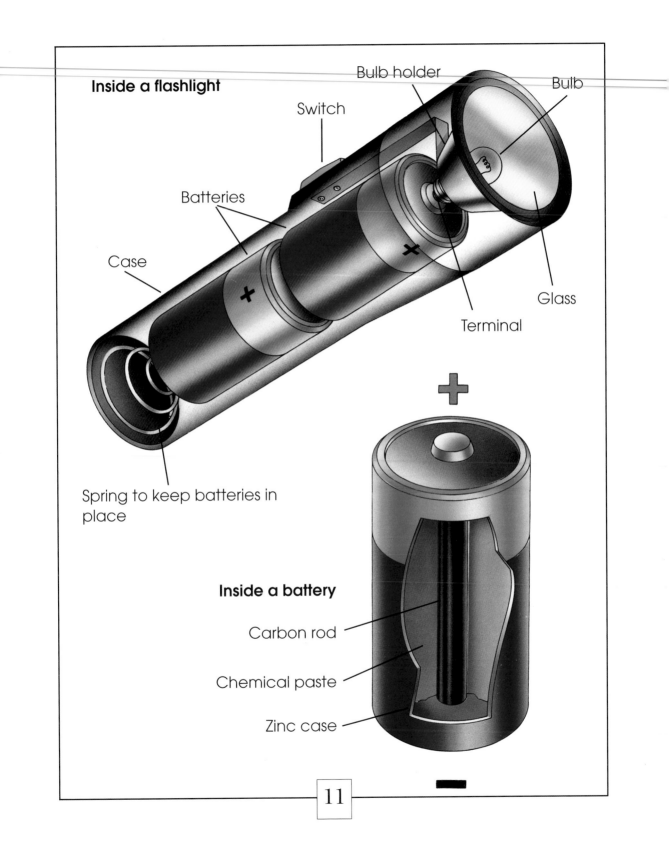

Inside a flashlight

Bulb holder

Bulb

Switch

Batteries

Case

Glass

Terminal

Spring to keep batteries in place

Inside a battery

Carbon rod

Chemical paste

Zinc case

11

Electrical Circuits – See for Yourself

A battery can light a bulb. It can only do this if there is something for the electricity to move through. Usually electricity moves through wires.

Electricity moves from a battery in one direction. It goes from the battery to the bulb. The bulb lights. Then the electricity flows back into the battery. The loop of wire the electricity flows through is called a circuit. The switch is like a gate or bridge. It opens and closes a gap in the circuit.

An electrical circuit

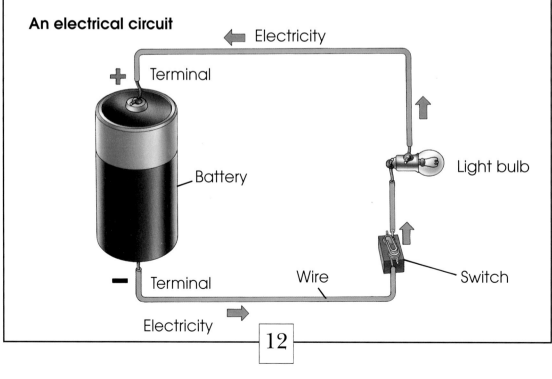

Not all materials let electricity flow through them. You can find out which materials let electricity flow through them with this circuit. Lay things made of wood, metal, paper, glass, and plastic across the thumbtacks. Some materials make the bulb light. Some materials stop the electricity so that the bulb does not light.

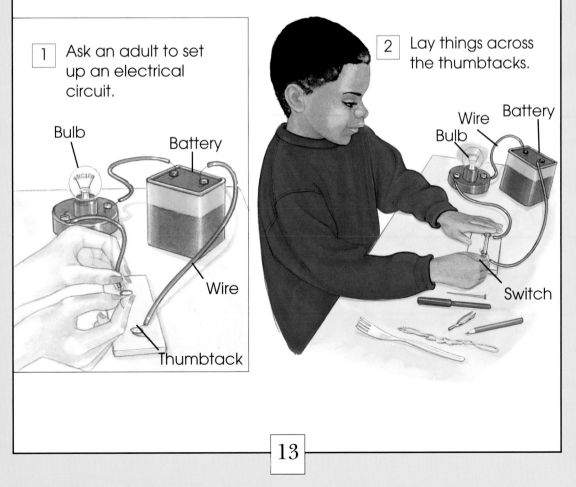

1 Ask an adult to set up an electrical circuit.

Bulb
Battery
Wire
Thumbtack

2 Lay things across the thumbtacks.

Wire
Battery
Bulb
Switch

Heat and Light from Electricity
See for Yourself

A light bulb has a thin wire inside it. This thin wire is called the filament. The electricity heats the filament. It makes the filament glow white hot. The glass bulb is filled with a special gas. This stops the filament from burning up too quickly.

An electric heater also has a thin coil of wire. Electricity flows through the wire. The wire gets red hot. It gives off heat.

Metal cap

Glass support

Wire to support filament

Gas

Filament

Filament of a light bulb magnified

You can see for yourself how electricity makes heat. Ask an adult to help you. Hammer two nails into a large cork. Wind a piece of thin copper wire neatly around a pencil. Gently slide the pencil out. The wire forms a coil. Attach this coil to the two nails.

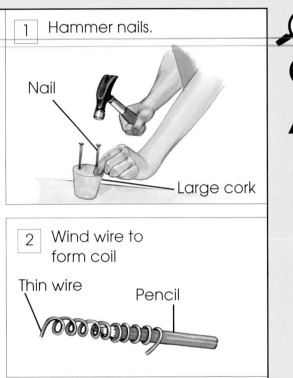

1 Hammer nails.

Nail

Large cork

2 Wind wire to form coil

Thin wire

Pencil

Connect the nails, battery, and switch with wires. Now the electricity flows through the circuit. **DO NOT** touch the coil. Put your finger *near* it. Can you feel the coil getting warm?

3 Make a circuit.

Battery

Switch

Coil of thin wire

In 1831 an English scientist, Michael Faraday, made an important discovery. When he moved a magnet near a coil of wire, electricity was produced.

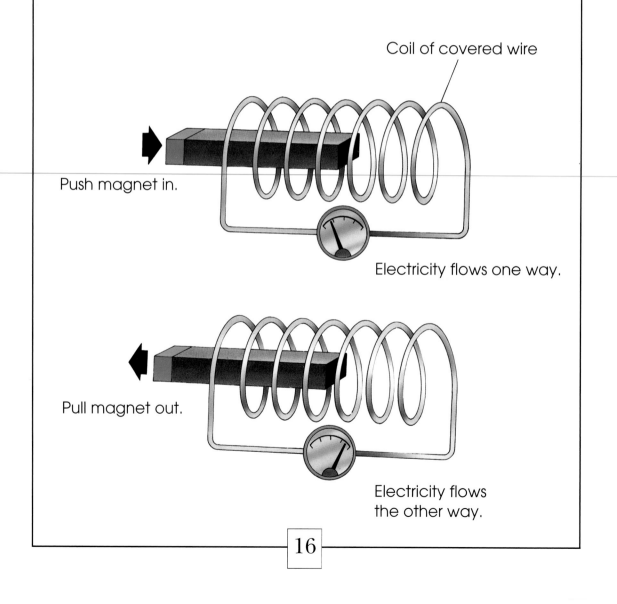

Coil of covered wire

Push magnet in.

Electricity flows one way.

Pull magnet out.

Electricity flows
the other way.

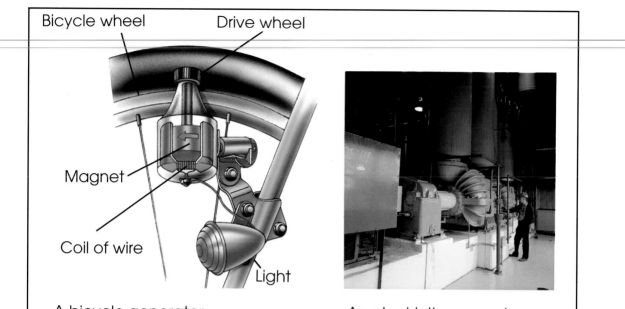

Bicycle wheel   Drive wheel

Magnet

Coil of wire

Light

A bicycle generator   An electricity generator

Today most of our electricity is produced using magnets. A bicycle generator set has a magnet inside a coil of wire. When the bicycle wheel goes around, it makes the magnet go around. This makes electricity flow and the lights work. Each of the generators at a power plant contains a magnet. When a generator turns, the magnet also turns inside a huge coil of wire. This produces the electricity we use every day.

Making Electricity
See for Yourself

You can produce electricity from a coil of wire. Find a cardboard tube 4 inches (10 cm) long. Ask an adult to cut two cardboard circles larger than the end of the tube. Ask an adult to cut a hole in the center of the circles. Glue a cardboard circle to each end to make a reel.

1 Cut hole in cardboard circle

Cardboard circles

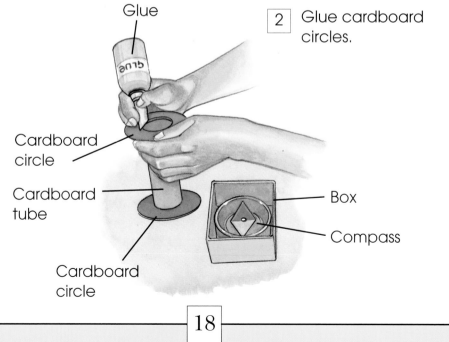

Glue

2 Glue cardboard circles.

Cardboard circle

Cardboard tube

Cardboard circle

Box

Compass

W ind thin, covered wire neatly and
evenly onto the reel. This is your coil.
Place a compass in a small box. Wrap thin,
covered wire neatly and evenly thirty times
around the box. Leave room at both ends,
so that you can see the compass needle.
Connect the wires. Move a bar magnet in
and out of the coil. The compass needle
will move as electricity is produced.

| 3 | Wind wire onto reel and box | 4 | Connect the wires. | 5 | Move magnet in and out. |

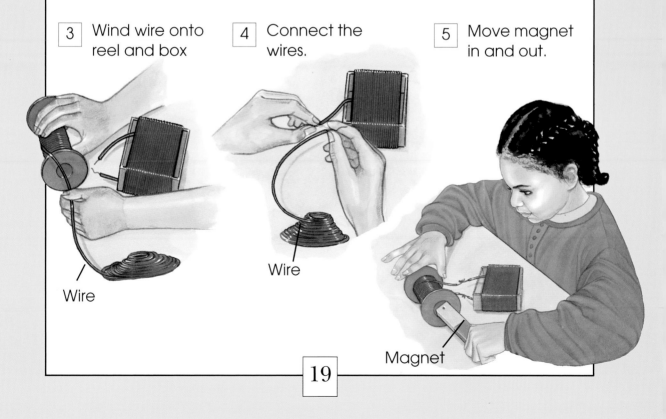

Wire

Wire

Magnet

Electric Motors

Electricity works all kinds of machines. Electric motors drive the fastest trains in the world. Electric motors also power vacuum cleaners and refrigerators. There are electric motors in washing machines and dishwashers. There are electric motors in food mixers, drills, and blow-dryers. Many cameras have tiny electric motors in them.

An electric drill

All electric motors have a magnet. They also have a coil of wire. When electricity flows in the coil, it pushes and pulls the magnet. These pushes and pulls make the motor spin. In some electric motors the magnet spins. In other motors the coil spins. The electric current goes into the motor through the commutator. The commutator changes the direction of the current every half turn, to keep the coil moving.

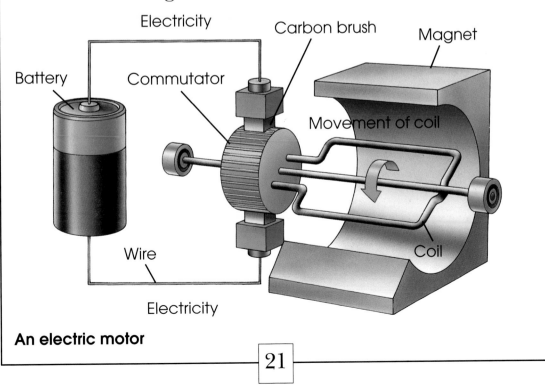

An electric motor

Electric Motors – See for Yourself

Use a magnet to see how an electric motor works. You need the lid from a pint ice cream carton. Put wire paper clips evenly all around the edge of the lid. Get the cap from a small tube of toothpaste. Glue the cap into the middle of the lid.

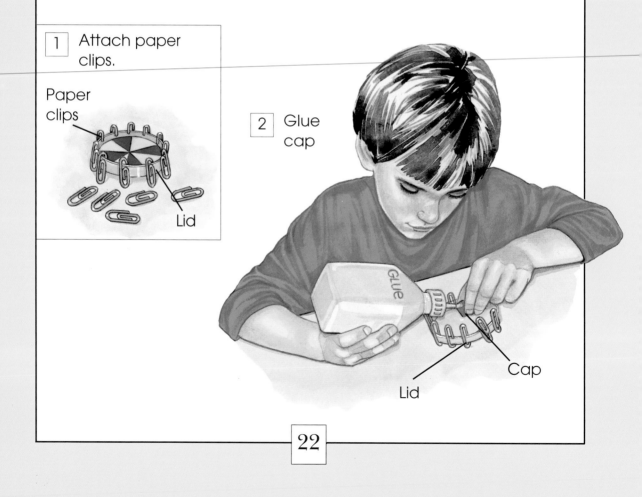

1   Attach paper clips.

Paper clips

Lid

2   Glue cap

Cap

Lid

Stick a lump of modeling clay to the table. Push a large sewing needle into the clay.

3 Push needle into clay

Sewing needle

Modeling clay

4 Balance toothpaste cap on needle

Sewing needle

Balance the toothpaste cap on the needle. Hold your magnet near one of the paper clips. Gently move the magnet around the lid. Can you make the lid spin?

5 Hold magnet near paper clip

Magnet

23

We have already seen some of the things magnets do. Magnets come in all shapes and sizes. Nearly all of them are made of iron or steel. Many of the things we use every day have magnets in them. Telephones, radios, electric clocks, and electric doorbells all have magnets. Electric motors and some door catches have magnets in them, too.

A magnet can pull or attract things made of iron to it. A magnet has the strongest pull at its ends. These ends are called the poles of the magnet.

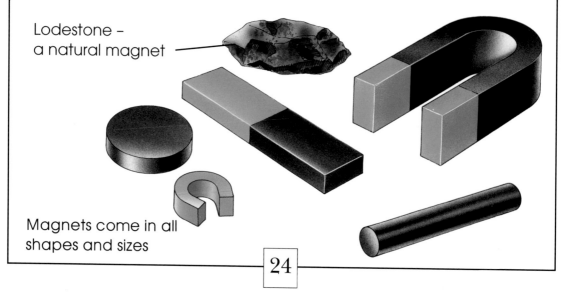

Lodestone – a natural magnet

Magnets come in all shapes and sizes

One end of a magnet is usually marked with a line, dot, or color. This end is called the north pole. The other end is the south pole. The north pole of one magnet will attract the south pole of another magnet. If two north poles or two south poles are placed together, the magnets push each other away.

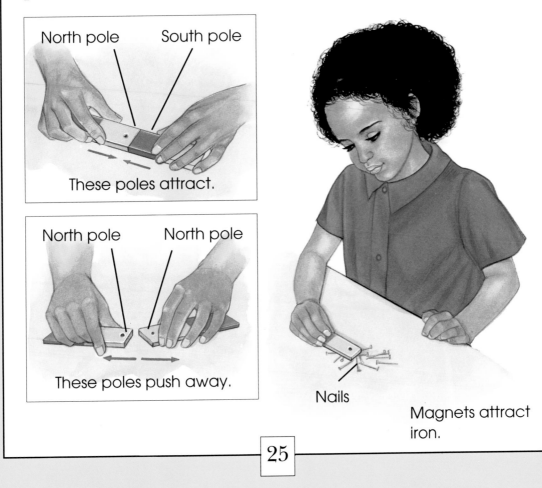

North pole   South pole

These poles attract.

North pole   North pole

These poles push away.

Nails

Magnets attract iron.

A compass is used to show direction. People walking in the mountains use a compass. Explorers use a compass. Ships and aircraft have compasses. The needle in a compass is a magnet. The needle always points to the north. Compasses work because the Earth is like a giant magnet.

Walking compass

Ship's compass

You can see for yourself how a compass works. Float a plastic lid in a dish of water. Carefully rest a bar magnet on the lid. The lid and the magnet will turn until one end of the magnet points north.

1 Float lid in water

Dish of water

Plastic lid

2 Rest a magnet on the lid.

Magnet

Plastic lid

Dish of water

Electromagnets

One kind of magnet uses electricity. It is called an electromagnet. An electromagnet will only attract iron and steel when the electricity is turned on. When the electricity is turned off, it is no longer a magnet. Junkyards use electromagnets. The electromagnets sort iron and steel from other metals. When the electricity is turned on, the magnet picks up pieces of iron and steel. When the electricity is turned off, the magnet drops these metals.

An electromagnet being used in a junkyard to sort metal

Many other machines have electromagnets in them. Electric doorbells, motors, and loudspeakers have electromagnets. Doctors can use an electromagnet to get steel splinters out of a person's eye. Trains that "float" above the tracks use electromagnets. There are electromagnets on the track and in the train. The magnets push against each other. Then the train can glide smoothly along.

Magnets make this train "float" above the track.

Electromagnets – See for Yourself

Make your own electromagnet. Wrap thin, covered wire neatly around a steel bolt. Ask an adult to strip the cover from the ends of the wire. Join the two ends of the wire to a battery. Hold one end of the bolt over a pile of nails. Then lift it up again. How many nails stick to the bolt?

Bolt

Wire

1 Wrap wire

Battery

Bolt

Wire

2 Join wire to battery

3 Hold bolt over nails

Nails

Glossary

Attract To pull something with a force that cannot be seen.

Battery A container filled with chemicals that act on each other. The chemicals produce electricity.

Cable A heavy, covered wire connecting power plants to electricity users.

Circuit The closed loop through which electricity flows.

Compass An instrument with a swinging needle (a magnet) that always points north. It is used to show direction.

Conductor Any material through which electricity can flow easily.

Electric motor A machine that changes electrical energy into movement energy.

Electricity A form of energy used for lighting, heating, and powering machines.

Electromagnet An iron bar surrounded by a coil of wire. It acts as a magnet when electricity flows through the wire.

Fuel Anything that is burned to make heat or power, such as coal, oil, gas, or wood.

Generator A machine for changing movement energy into electrical energy.

Insulator Any material that will not allow electricity to flow.

Iron A hard, gray metal from which steel is made.

Magnet A piece of iron or steel that will pick up or attract smaller pieces of iron or steel.

Power plant A large building where electricity is produced.

Pylon A metal tower that carries electricity cables or wires.

Steel A tough, hard metal made of iron and carbon. Steel is used to make cars, machines, tools, and nails.

Switch A device for turning electricity on and off.

Turbine A kind of engine that is turned by air, gas, water, or steam.

Utility pole A pole that carries electricity cables or wires.

Index